CATHOLIC WOMEN:
Carriers Of
LIVING WATER
To a WORLD
that Thirsts for
PEACE

I0142301

By
Dr. Rose U. Mezu

Black Academy Press, Inc.

CATHOLIC WOMEN: CARRIERS OF LIVING WATER TO A WORLD THAT THIRSTS FOR PEACE

By

DR. ROSE URE MEZU

CATHOLIC WOMEN:
CARRIERS OF LIVING WATER
TO A WORLD THAT THIRSTS FOR PEACE

BY
DR. ROSE URE MEZU

First Edition 2018
Published by
Black Academy Press, Inc.

Catholic Women, Living Water, Bible, Catholicism, Feminism

ISBN 0-87831-001-0   Paper   9780878310012

FIRST EDITION

BLACK ACADEMY PRESS, INC.
4015 OLD COURT ROAD
BALTIMORE, MARYLAND 21208 USA

DEDICATION

To

All Catholic Women who are
Carriers of Living Water
My Mother Bessie Chiege Iwuji Okeke
All Mothers in my Family
In Our Lady of Mt. Carmel Catholic Parish, Emekuku, Imo
State, Nigeria
In St. Charles Borromeo Catholic Church, Pikesville,
Maryland, USA;
and above all
To the Gentle Woman, Mary,
Model of Catholic Women And
The Original and Only Carrier of
The Eternal Source of Living Water.

CATHOLIC WOMEN:
CARRIERS OF LIVING WATER
TO A WORLD THAT THIRSTS FOR PEACE

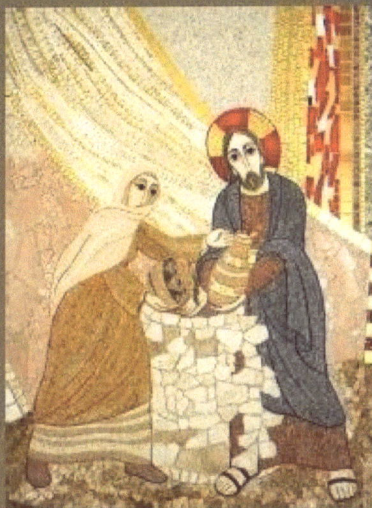

Members of Our Lady of Mount Carmel
Catholic Church Food Kitchen, Emekeukwu,
Nigeria 2018

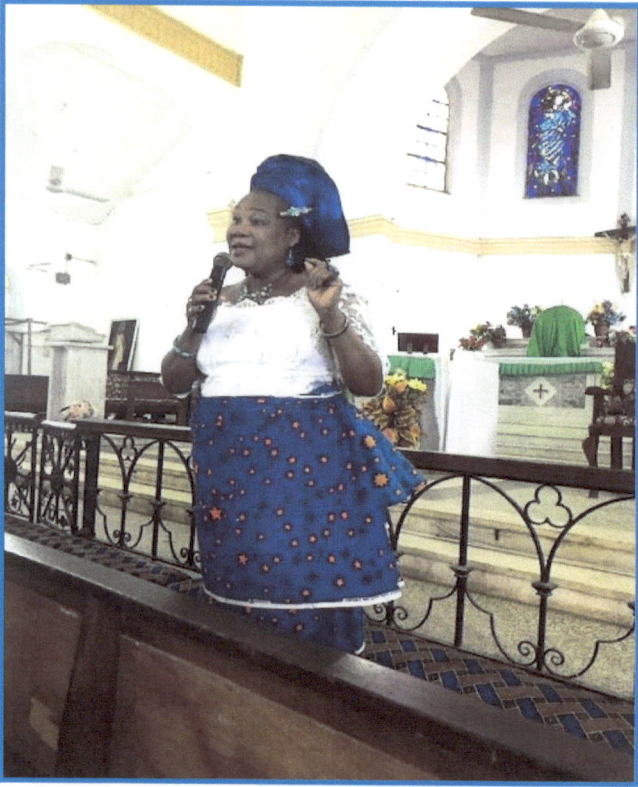

**Dr. Rose Ure Mezu Addressing the
Congregation After Mass**

At Mt. Carmel Catholic Church, Emekeukwu,

Owerri Arhdiocese, Nigeria

Christian Mothers

*Our Lady of Mt. Carmel Catholic Church,
Emekeukwu, Nigeria*

Contents

FOREWORD

CATHOLIC WOMEN:
CARRIERS OF LIVING WATER
TO A WORLD THAT THIRSTS FOR PEACE

Being a lecture delivered to Christian Mothers of Our Lady of
Mount Carmel Catholic Parish, Emekeukwu on the occasion of
the Mother's Day Retreat
Holden on Thursday, April 5, 2018.

*"To be Generous is to draw from the Living Waters and Give to
others to Drink so they may live!"*
-- Dr. Rose Ure Mezu.

*One starving person telling another starving person where to find
bread." Demonstration of God's love should not be merely
Abstract."*
--- Bishop Robert Barron.

*"Let nothing disturb you, let nothing frighten you. All things
pass. God Alone does not change. Patience achieves everything.
Whoever has God lacks nothing; God Alone Is Sufficient."*
— St. Teresa of Avila.

*The woman said, "'I know that Messiah" (called Christ) "is
coming. When he comes, he will   explain everything to us.'
Then Jesus declared, 'I, the one speaking to you—I am he.'"*

--(*John* 4: 25-26).

The State of Our World: What is wrong with it?

This Mothers' Day Retreat Theme, "**Catholic Women: Carriers of Living Water to a World that Thirsts for Peace**," examines several concepts, viz: Why the World lacks Peace, the kind of Peace it is thirsting for, the definition and signification of **Living Water**, who Catholic Women are, and the Role of Catholic Women as Carriers of Living Water to a thirsty World.

God is the Source of Living Water. And anyone of any gender, and any age who is infused with Grace can be a Carrier of Living Water. This Living Water is the **saving** Water that brings Eternal Life. **Nothing else can quench human thirst except Living Water from this Eternal Source.** *Psalm* 42 captures this unquenchable **Thirst** so well: "*As the deer pants for streams of water, so my soul pants for you, my God. My soul thirsts for God, for the Living God. When Shall I See You face to face?*" *A*nd *Psalm* 23 attests to the revivifying quality of Living Water: "Near restful waters He leads me / to revive my drooping spirit!"

Also, we are reminded that from the very beginning, "biblical theology has shown us water as an invigorating element of nature…which is presented…[as] covering the expanse of the earth (cf. Gen 1:2). It is from water that all other beings come into existence. We will say in ordinary language that "water is life" -- (WUCWO Woman, carrier of "living water" - Jacqueline Maboul Mindja). It is only by the grace of Living Water that Peace can be brought to a world that is thirsting for

Peace, and we Catholic Women are the carriers of this Living Water.

Therefore, our Mothers' Day Lenten / Easter Retreat Reflection / Conversation will attempt to identify the Source of Living Water, examine the essential qualities, or Virtues that can guarantee not just Catholic Women but other sinful human beings a drink of this **Living Water** that revives, cleanses, heals, quenches thirst and guarantees us a share of divine life with our Triune God. Emphasis will be on the *Virtues of Trust (Faith), Patience, Humility, Obedience,* **and** *Love* as indispensable requirements to procuring this Living Water.

Today, our World is in a mess. There are wars in many countries of the World: In Africa - Sudan, Egypt, Libya, Congo, Central African Republic, *et cetera;* there are ongoing civil wars, wars between African nations, secessionist and separatist conflicts, national violence, riots and massacres, making Africa a theater of war. In the Middle East – Israelis and Palestinians are embroiled in an endless War that has killed millions, and maimed many more; so also in other parts of Middle East and Asia - Turkey, and Myanmar (Burma), in parts of Europe, in Venezuela and other parts of South America, and in many other countries. In these war-torn areas, people are being bombed and displaced from their homes and several generations of children have known no other home but Refugee camps. All over the world, there are terrorist attacks on towns and cities, creating instability and fear.

In the United States of America, young children are

carrying military assault weapons, going into schools, movie theaters, concert venues, and malls, *et al*, shooting other young people. On Saturday, March 23, 2018, young people all over America (and sympathizers all over the world, including African children) marched to the Capital, Washington, D. C. to say to their Government, to their Lawmakers, to their gun-loving parents and other adults: "Enough is Enough! We do not want to die young. It is about our lives. Ban the assault weapons, the guns, and if the legislators do not, we will vote them out come Mid-term Elections in November 2018."

Also, in many parts of the world, children are dying from starvation, whole villages are being wiped out by earthquakes, hurricanes, Tsunamies, creating millions of orphans. Igbo Catholic Women whose families fought the Nigeria–Biafran War, know all about Starvation, bombs and destruction. One Million Biafrans died. Dr. Sebastian Okechukwu Mezu recorded the complex intrigues, and horrors of the Biafran Tragedy in his 1970 novel, *Behind the Rising Sun*. Igbo people can also say along with the world's hurting youth: "Never Again! - Enough is Enough!" Then, in our own country Nigeria, in our states, and communities, there is no peace, no good or compassionate government; workers and pensioners are suffering, dying from not being paid their earned salaries; young University graduates have no employment; and in homes, and families, parents are even struggling contentiously with their own children, there are constant quarrels, fights; there are armed robberies, kidnappings, the ravages of *Boko Haram,* and the *Terrorism of Fulani Cattle Herdsmen.* So, it can safely be said that our World is in a state of Anomy and *Disharmony.* Our world truly is thirsting for Peace, the kind of Peace the world cannot give.

When one is thirsty, the person looks for a drink, more commonly for Water. *"Water, Water Everywhere and Not any drop to Drink,"* so goes a line in Samuel Taylor Coleridge's "Rime of the Ancient Mariner." The ancient Mariner (sailor) was at Sea, dying of Thirst, but could not find safe, drinkable water – only salty, harmful sea water. Water, Water, Water! Where would we be without It? We often take it for granted! Our bodies have a 70% Water content; our brain surface is mainly water. Indeed, we need water for many other purposes: we use water to cook food that nourish our body; we use water to bathe, to wash clothes and utensils; we use water to grow plants, and food. Rain water nourishes the Earth so we do not have droughts and famines.

Besides, millions of women and children around the world cover long distances, carrying water pitchers to fetch water. Especially women, biological nurturers and homemakers, can be labeled "water carriers" in rural villages as they keep their families alive, fed and healthy. *No Water, No Growth!*

Now, when there is an outbreak of Fire, what do we do? We rush for Water to quench it. And when we are thirsty, what do we do? We Drink water. And if we do not find water to drink, we keep panting and searching like the Deer, for *Something' to quench our Thirst, to fill up the deep, gaping Void in our troubled, lonely, hungry, Thirsty, tortured souls so we can have Peace* - a Peace that is actually a spiritual Hunger and which can only be assuaged by not just ordinary water, but Living Water - the subject of this Retreat Reflection.

Living Water *is Running Water, is active Water. Water is supposed to flow, to run, and Not to stay stagnant.* Therefore, for our Souls, we need active, Living Water: The Bible is replete with so many references to Living Water that is an active, nourishing, running and Healing water.

Just a few examples will suffice: When the Angel of God took Ezekiel to see Water flowing from the right side of the Temple, the Angel sat Ezekiel down on the bank of what has now swollen to become a River, and Ezekiel testifies: "He said to me,

'*This water flows into the eastern district down upon the Arabah, and empties into the sea, the salt waters, which it makes fresh. Wherever the river flows, every sort of living creature that can multiply shall live, and there shall be abundant fish, for wherever this water comes, the sea shall be made fresh. Along both banks of the river, fruit trees of every kind shall grow; their leaves shall not fade, nor their fruit fail. Every month they shall bear fresh fruit, for they shall be watered by the flow from the sanctuary. Their fruit shall serve for food, and their leaves for medicine.*" ---(*Ezekiel* 47: 9, 12).

Equally, *Psalm* One (1) blesses the person who follows the law of the Lord and keeps His commandments, who *"is like a tree <u>planted by streams of running water / that yields its fruit in its season, / and its leaves do not wither; in whatever he does, he prospers.</u>*

And *Psalm* 23 tells us "*Near restful Waters, He leads me, to Revive my Drooping Spirit.*"

All these are references to Water that is living, healing, restful and guarantees Peace. Therefore, all shall be well with the World **Only** If human beings Can have Peace.

* * * *

But Why Is the World Not at Peace?

A. Biblical References - Creation

Genesis states that after the job of Creation, "God looked at everything he had made, and he was very pleased"_(*Genesis* 1: 31}.

Psalm **8** equally sings the Creator Lord's praises, exclaiming,

How Excellent is Thy Name, O Lord, my God!

When I think of the heavens, the work of Your hands: the moon and the stars, which You have made; /

What is man, that thou art mindful of him?

Mortal man, that You care for him? /

For You have made him a little lower than the angels, and with glory and honor, You have crowned him. /

And given him Dominion *over the works of Your hands; You have put all things under his feet - All sheep and oxen, yea, even to the savage beasts of the field, /*

the birds that fly in the air, the fish that swim in the sea./

O, Lord, our God, how Excellent is Thy Name
in all the earth! (Psalm 8: 3-9).

So, Creator God meant for All living
in the world to be happy!
And yet, we are Not! And Yet the World has No Peace.

But Why? For an explanation, we go back to the
beginning of human life – Creation.
The Bible tells us that when God created the first
human being – Adam, He gave him a companion Eve
– bone of his bone, and flesh of his flesh, and bestowed on
them the Garden of Eden and told them to eat freely of all
the trees in the garden, except for the tree of the knowledge
of good and evil.

But Adam and Eve listened to the seductive
reasoning of the Serpent who said,

"You will not certainly die….
For God knows that, when you eat from it,
your eyes will be opened, and you will be like God,
knowing good and evil."

And, seeking to be Equal with God, they fell from
Grace, and thus lost their Innocence and Purity.
No longer pure, they now discovered that they
were naked; so, they hid themselves, since now

they can distinguish good from evil.

I say to you that the capital Sin of Adam and Eve is a
Lack of Trust that led to Pride, and Arrogance,
a lack of Humility and Obedience. Lacking Trust and
Humility, they became Greedy, Prideful, and
so sought to be like God.

We remember that the Archangel that drove Lucifer
and his bad angels out of Heaven is called
Mica El (Hebrew = Mikha'el = Who is like God?
His name is merely a Question "Who is like God?).
Indeed, nobody is like God, and neither would
Adam and Eve be God.

Consequently, when Yahweh called to the man,

"Where are you?"
Adam answered,
"I heard you in the garden, and I was afraid
because I was naked; so I hid."

And He asked,
"Who told you that you were naked?
Have you eaten from the tree
that I commanded you not to eat from?"

The man said,
"The woman you put here with me –
she gave me some fruit from the tree, and I ate it."

Then the Lord God said to the woman,
"What is this you have done?"

The woman said,
"The serpent deceived me, and I ate."

So the Lord God said to the serpent,
"Because you have done this:
"I will make your pains
in childbearing very severe;
with painful labor you will give birth to children....

To Adam, He said,
"Because you ... ate fruit from the tree
about which I commanded you,
'You must not eat from it,'
"... all the days of your life....

By the sweat of your brow,
you will eat your food until you return to the ground
since from it you were taken;
for dust you are and to dust you will return."

And thus, Death entered into the world.
Adam named his wife "Eve" because
she would become the mother of all the living....

So the Lord God banished him from
the Garden of Eden to work the ground
from which he had been taken."

- Holy Bible, (NIV), 2011.

It is worthy of notice that God did not buy Adam's excuse of Eve as the Tempter; nor did God accept Eve heaping the blame on the serpent. He punished both of them. Every created being is autonomous, God is saying, and is therefore responsible for one's actions. And every Act has consequences. Of all religions, Christianity is the Only One that judges man and woman equally.

In Islam, for instance, the man speaks for the woman, same as in the Jewish Religion. Women would sit at the back of the Temple, or, stay home and the man hears and interprets the words of the Rabbi for his wife.

In *Christianity, Salvation is personal*. Each human being speaks for ONESELF and is rewarded or condemned accordingly.

Thus, because of the lack of Trust, Humility and Obedience shown by Adam and Eve, Death entered into the Life of human beings – Life that was meant to be pure, lovely, *INNOCENT, and PERFECT – JUST LIKE God. And Adam and Eve lost this Purity and Perfection out of a lack of TRUST!*

Thus began the subsequent Story of human Encounter with God. This Encounter will not be notable by our search for God, but by God's Love and Mercy that impel His search, indeed the relentless Pursuit of human beings right to the Limit of God-Forsaken-ness – into our world of sin and injustice. God's unending pursuit of us is to bring human beings back to the happiness originally meant for His creatures.

It is like Francis Thompson's mystical poem about the pursuit of the deer by the Hound of Heaven. It is like the Father's Search for the lost Prodigal Son. The Prodigal Father can be said to have the same endless Source of mercy / compassion, and love which God the Father has for us, for, upon sighting his lost son from afar, the old King actually runs to meet, embrace him and throw a feast for him, because as the Father explains to the older son, "He was lost but now he has been found; he was dead and Now he is alive!" Likewise, despite our constant disobedience and turning away, God still pursues to get us back, out of love.

B. Additional Biblical References - Abraham

So, from the beginning of Creation, the Lord God wanted HUMAN BEINGS TO HAVE ETERNAL LIFE, BE HAPPY, AND, BE WITH HIM. He made the world to be beautiful, rich and pleasurable. We have seen how our first parents squandered that Grace. What Virtues did they lack? We have talked about Trust. Another virtue to emphasize is Humility. *"Humility, Humility, Humility,"* says St. Faustyna – *it is a Primary virtue. With Humility come Obedience and Trust.*

Now, comes a man of God who knew and Trusted God. Abraham, the Man from Ur, was given the same divine Favor as Adam. And Abraham, like Adam, was also Severely Tested to the point of being asked to *sacrifice his, and Sarah's Only Son of Promise:*

"Then God said, 'Take your son, your only son, whom you love—Isaac—and go to the region of Moriah. Sacrifice him there as a burnt offering on a mountain I will show you.'" So, Abraham took his Son Isaac and set out in obedience.

And when Isaac asked: "Father ... "'but where is the

lamb for the burnt offering?'

Abraham answered, 'God himself will provide the lamb for the burnt offering, my son."

Abraham knew God's providential wealth and said it:

"The Lord will Provide!"

Next, an Angel of God calls out, "Abraham! Abraham!... Do not lay a hand on the boy," he said. "Do not do anything to him." And Having found Abraham worthy, the Lord did provide a substitute - a ram (animal) in place of Isaac (human being), thus showing his omnipotence and vast mercy.

And God spoke to Abraham a second time:

Now I know that you fear God...I swear by myself, that because you ... have not withheld your son, your only son. I will surely bless you and make your descendants as numerous as the stars in the sky and as the sand on the seashore...through your offspring, all nations on earth will be blessed because you have obeyed me." (*Genesis*: 1-19)

Therefore, Obedience, Trust, Humility – these mean – Love, for God.

Abraham Trusted Yahweh, and Knew that He is a God of love, power and mercy, a Source of Living Water – Graces, and a God Who keeps His every Promise, for after all, He had promised him a son with Sara in their very old age and had God kept that promise. Therefore, I say to you that Abraham demonstrated Humility that comes from that Trust. @AmandaNwaba (my granddaughter) was wondering in confusion what at all is admirable about Abraham trying to kill his son Isaac. And my answer to her is my answer to you: that deep within his heart, Abraham did not believe that his son Isaac would die. Out of Humility, he did not falter in Obedience, and Knowing already that he could Trust God's word, that God was putting him to the Severest test, yet, he obeyed God's Will. Similarly, Isaac meekly and trustingly obeyed his Father Abraham, and lay down to be sacrificed; yet, Isaac knew deep in his heart that his Father, loving him, would never harm him, just as Abraham knew that God is Full of mercy and love. Abraham, symbolically, is a carrier of Living Water - God's Grace. With God, Source of Living Water, Love is all about Trust and Obedience! Conversely, there is another man of God who at one point in his ministry lacked Trust - Moses.

C. Biblical References to Living Water: Moses

There was no water for the Hebrew community in the desert of Meribah, and so the people rose in opposition, grumbling against Moses and Aaron saying,

If only we had died when our brothers fell dead before the Lord! Why did you bring the Lord's community into this wilderness, that we and our livestock should die here? Why did you bring us up out of Egypt to this terrible place? It has no grain, or figs, grapevines or pomegranates. And there is no water to drink!

The Lord instructed Moses to raise his hand and Strike the Rock **Once** to give life-sustaining Water to the Israelites in the desert. The people grumbled again. Moses did so. For the second time, God asked him not to

Strike, but to speak to the rock to yield its water: *"Take the staff, and . . . gather the assembly together. **Speak to that rock** before their eyes and it will pour out its water ... so they and their livestock can drink."* (*Numbers* 20: 8-12)

But Moses lacked Trust and Obedience; he lacked Patience and Humility, too; and so, he strikes a second time instead of Speaking to the Rock in the Lord's name. He did not Trust that One Strike alone will do it. *Moses totally failed to trust God for the life-supplying water. He tried to take matters into his own hands. He was supposed to be the leader, but he was also the servant of God. He did Not OBEY God's order. Like Adam and Eve, he too tried to usurp God's place, and f*or that, he was punished.

God dispensed his judgment. From afar, Moses could look upon the promised Land, but he would not enter it; Joshua, the son of Nun would lead the Hebrews into the Promised Land, that Land flowing with milk and honey which Yahweh had promised Abram, the man from Ur in Mesopotamia, whom the Lord God renamed Abraham. At the end, Moses lacked the Trust, Patience, Humility and the Obedience of Abraham, and of another woman, the Widow of Zarephath, near the Phoenician city of Sidon (Kings 17 : 7- 16). Obedience and Trust are important to the Eternal Source of Living Water.

D. Biblical References: Elijah and the Widow of Zarephtha

In a period of drought and Famine in the Kingdom of Ahab (the wicked king of Israel), the prophet Jeremiah asked her for food: "Please," he said, "bring me a little water in a cup so that I may drink." When she went to get him drink, Elijah added: "Please, bring me a piece of bread." (1 Ki. 17:10,11). Giving the stranger a drink did not trouble the widow but giving him bread was a problem.

"As surely as Jehovah your God is living," she replied, "I have no bread, only a handful of flour in the large jar and a little oil in the small jar. Now I am gathering a few pieces of wood, and I will go in and make something for me and my son. After we have eaten, we will die." (1 Kings 17:12)

Yet, Elijah asked her to prepare bread for him. She obeyed. And because she obeyed, Jehovah multiplied her meager supplies and the widow never lacks oil, or flour until the famine ends. In addition, Elijah also saves and brings back to life her dead son. With "Trust and Obedience," we gain Everything else. Trust and Obey, says the Lord!

Ah, yes, again, the capital Virtue that controls all others is TRUST! With Trust (Faith) follows Humility, Patience, and Obedience - Acceptance of God's Will – a belief that God Knows All Things, Is the Source of All Things, Can Do All Things, Loves us, and Will Never let Evil befall anyone who is Humble enough to Trust and Obey. Abraham and the widow of Zarephtha are thus the embodiment of the Trust, Patience, Humility and Obedience that Adam, Eve, and Moses did not have.

They also are Carriers of Living Water (Grace).

Analogously, we can say that, because the Lord God loves human beings and wants them to be with HIM, *Very Special Alternative Persons have to be provided who will Willingly do God's Will: a New Eve, and a New Adam = Mary is the New Eve, and Son of God, Jesus – the New Adam.* Yes, Jesus, Second Person of the Trinity, although fully God, will be enfleshed, be born and is also to be fully Man. As Man, he had Trust, Obedience, Humility and followed God's Will of *Sacrifice of Himself for human Redemption.* Thus, Love is Not Love, without Sacrifice.

* * * *

Catholic Women and Mary of Galilee – Mentor:

And Who are Catholic Women?

To Know who is a Catholic Christian Woman, we must go to that very special Woman whom the *Lord God chose as the New Eve - Mary of Galilee, who more than any human being, dead, living, or yet to be born, embodies all the virtues that Symbolize Absolute Love for our Trinitarian God. Mary will become a* Carrier of the Source of Living Water.

Yet, Mary was a very young girl just like other young girls of her hometown; she lived out her goodness and godliness unaware that from the beginning of Salvation History, she had been specially prepared for the highest honor any human being can receive – to be Immaculate, free from original Sin for she is to become Mother to the Son of God – *Theotokos* – God-Bearer, Vessel of Honor, of the New Covenant between created Human beings and the God of Creation.

This is Mary's Special Charism – to become the Mother of the Lamb of God Who would be born fully Man for, He would live, hunger, thirst, and suffer like any man would, and, by giving up His Life on the wood of the Cross, He will continue God's Love-Pursuit of His created beings to bring them back into friendship with their Creator.

Likewise, like Mary, not one of us is useless; each of us

has a **Special Mission, Charism**, or Gift and has been destined for something special. Blessed Cardinal John Henry Newman says it better:

"God has created me to do Him some definite service. He has committed some work to me which He has not committed to another. I have my mission.... Therefore, I will Trust Him, whatever I am...."

If we listen closely to, and follow the voice of the Lord that speaks in our heart, we will discover what our Mission in life is. Just as the young Mary of Galilee did. She must have been immersed in prayer when she saw the Angel Gabriel (Strength of God = *IkeChukwu*- Igbo) who from an Invisible Dimension of Existence made himself Visible, calling out in Greeting,

"*Hail Mary, Full of Grace, the Lord is with You!*"

ArchAngel Raphael greeted Mary with the very Virtue that Adam and Eve had foolishly, and pridefully thrown away. ArchAngel Gabriel calls her, "full of Grace." Now what is **Grace**? I would say, Resplendent Purity … See-through Translucence, Perfection – the very quality needed to see God. The ArchAngel went on:

"The Lord is with You!"

If the Lord is with her, then the Lord is Already within Mary.

"And she was troubled at his saying and cast in her mind what manner of salutation this should be.

And the angel said unto her,

"Fear not, Mary: for thou hast found favor with God.

And, behold, thou shalt conceive in thy womb, and bring forth a son, and shalt call his name Jesus" -= *Joshua, Yeshua (Hebrew).*

Confused, Mary asked the angel,

"How Can this be, seeing I know not man?"

The Angel explains:

"The Holy Spirit shall come upon you and the Power of the Most High will overshadow you. You will conceive in your womb and bear a Son and you shall call his name Emmanuel - the Lord with you. He shall be great and shall be called the Son of the Most High, and the Lord God shall give unto him the throne of his father David: And he shall reign over the house of Jacob forever; and of his kingdom, there shall be no end."

Then, the Angel also gives Mary an example of an Impossibility that has become possible, saying:

"And, behold, thy cousin Elisabeth, she hath also conceived a son in her old age: and this is the sixth month with her, who was called barren, for with God nothing shall be impossible."

And Mary said, ***"Behold, I am the handmaid of the Lord; Let it Be done unto me according to thy word."***

This is Mary's ***Fiat – Let it be done!*** Let the Will of God be done! She says, "Yes" of her own Volition!

Feminist Ideology says that every action should be the individual's free, and personal Decision. Mary willingly, without being forced, agrees to become the New Eve. She agrees to be Carrier of the Source of

Living Water by which all sins - the sins of Adam and Eve, and Humankind will be washed away. She will be Carrier of the very Source of Living Water, who will be born as a mortal Man, of the same substance as the Father and the Holy Spirit – Divine, and yet fully human without any co-mingling of Substances divine and mortal: able to feel hungry, be thirsty, tired, to feel pain, suffer and die just like any human being. As fully Man, He will be the Lamb of God, the Sacrificial Lamb that will fulfill the Promise Yahweh made to David – that his royal line will rule forever. After generations of David's descendants proved unable to follow the commandments of God in Spirit and in Truth, Yahweh will send His own Anointed Son, the Christ-to-be-King forever, out of David's lineage through Joseph the carpenter, husband of Mary. This will mark the height of God's Love-Pursuit - the promise of Eternal Love. Even when human beings have sinned and do not deserve love, compassion and mercy, yet God loves, and is compassionate, and will Cleanse with not just Water but indeed with the very Blood of His Only Begotten Son wash away all human Sins – past, present and Future. How then Can we Not Love such a Lover! And who again is the Carrier of this very Source of Living Water – *Mary of Galilee, Theotokos - God-Bearer,* First, and greatest Disciple, First Christian Mother, First Christian Woman under whose aegis (protection) fall all other women.

And the young Mary, did she fully understand the full scope of the Will of God – what, God through the Archangel Gabriel was asking of her. I will say to you, "No!" At Annunciation, she did not understand fully the complexity and mystery of what she was asked to undertake; but She did not doubt like the priest Zacharia;

she only wondered how this could happen.

Yes, **Mary of Galilee had Humility; she had Trust, therefore Obedience, and was ready to willingly do God's Will**: *"Behold, I am the handmaid of the Lord. Let it be done to me according to Thy Will."* And we know from St. Maria Faustyna, that God's holy Will is but "Love and Mercy, Itself." Just as when the Apostles asked the LORD Jesus to teach them to pray, Jesus, the New Adam, taught them the "Our Father..." In this prayer is the line, **"Thy Will be done, on Earth as it is in Heaven."** At the Garden of Gethsemane, Jesus shuddered at the painful passion he would undergo, but said, **"Not my Will, but Thy Will be Done!"** At the Cross, the very Source of Living Water said: "I Thirst!" Rather than Water, He was scornfully given Vinegar to drink and when He had completed His Mission on Earth, Jesus said, "It is Finished!" To do the Will of God, The Source of Living Water, requires Trust, Patience, humility, Obedience to the Father – all the components parts of true Love.

Continuing with the Trope of Living Water

When John the Baptizer saw Jesus, the Source of Living Water, he refused to baptize Him, but Jesus insisted so that "all righteousness shall be fulfilled." Being fully Man, Jesus obeyed the law according to Tradition. But John identifies and proclaims the Lord God to the people, "Behold the Lamb of God!... I am not worthy to untie the straps of His sandal! I baptize you with water but He will baptize you with fire and the Holy Spirit."

* * * *

The Woman of Samaria

"Who is the Source of Living Water?"

Women's Voice

Official Magazine of the World Union of Catholic Women's Organisations

November 2017 - N° 44

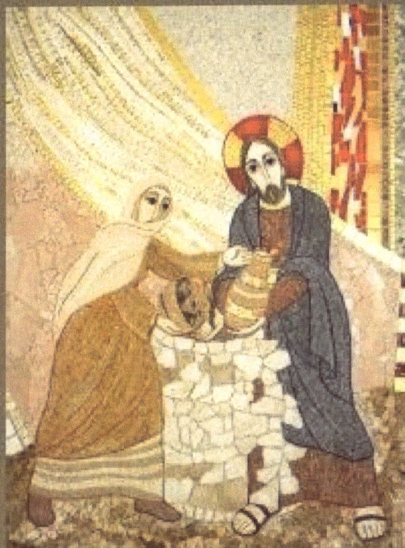

WUCWO Women, Carriers of "living water" to a world which thirsts for Peace

World Union of Catholic Women's Organisations * Union Mondiale des Organisations Féminines Catholiques
Unión Mundial de las Organizaciones Femeninas Católicas * Weltunion Katholischer Frauenorganisationen

He who Walks on the Waters of the Sea, Who Calms the Storms with a word, He of Whom it is asked, "What manner of man is this that even the winds and the Sea obey Him?" He is the Ocean of unfathomable Divine Mercy. He is the Source of Living Waters – the Lord God Almighty, Unbounded, UnCreated, Omniscient, and Omnipresent in a Trinitarian Union with the Father and the Holy Spirit.

Jesus meets the Woman of Samaria at Jacob's Well in Sychar. From all accounts, the Woman of Samaria was not a virtuous woman. Because she was a figure of Scandal, in fact, a prostitute, she would not go to the Well early in the day, or at sundown, but chose to go at Mid-day, when the Sun is at its hottest and so no people would be at the well, perhaps, to avoid gossip and ill-treatment by fellow women, and men.

So, she came alone: and Jesus also came Alone, unaccompanied. Other Jews would bypass that territory because they hold Samaritans in contempt as apostates - unbelievers, and half-breeds, and would not talk to them. But Jesus is the Lord who crosses all boundaries, Who visits those at the margins of society (the woman caught in adultery, Mary Magdalene), Who welcomes those despised and those shunned such as the Publican, Tax Collectors (Levi, Zaccheus), and others cast out of the society such as Lepers. So, Jesus started talking to the Samaritan woman who was surprised that a Jew was talking to her. Besides, being a man, he should not be seen speaking in public with any woman, much less a public sinner. Bishop Robert Barron says this encounter shows that Jesus as Divine Mercy is in relentless pursuit of human beings. He will Never give up because he loves human beings, wants to make us sharers in the

Divine Life and also because "*'Gloria Dei est Homo vivens'* - The glory of God is a human being fully alive" as stated by Iraeneus, second Century theologian:

The glory of God is Jesus .... Jesus is how God chose to reveal God's glory most definitively... so in Jesus, the glory of God is a human being fully alive. The more we become like Jesus, the more we begin to reveal God's glory too. – Taylor Marshall. - http://taylormarshall.com/2013/04/the-glory-of-god-is-man-fully-alive-did.html

Therefore, God became Man so that we may become God. God wants to divinize us – make us like Him – holy and Perfect: "**Be you Perfect as my Heavenly Father is Perfect!**" That is the Lord Jesus' earthly Mission – to make us Clean, purified, made Whole and Sin-free, i.e. Perfect. *"Wash me and I shall be clean,"* says *Psalm* 51. Then, we can be filled with Living Water. But the only way we can be filled with eternal Living Water is by emptying ourselves of all addictions, allowing ourselves to be washed, purified, made Clean by Living Water from an Eternal Source.

So, Jesus gets on with His Mission – the quest / pursuit of love, and, says to the Woman of Samaria,

"Will you Give me a drink?" When she resists, citing the customary Jewish taboos, Jesus says to her:

"If you only knew the gift of God, and who it is that say to you, 'Give me to drink'; you would have asked of him, and he would have given you living water. "

"Sir," the woman said, "you have nothing to draw with, and the well is deep. Where can you get this living water ...?"

Jesus answered, *"Everyone who drinks this water will be thirsty again, but whoever drinks the water I give them will never thirst. Indeed, the water I give them will become in them a Spring of water welling up to eternal life."*

And the woman said to him, *"Sir, give me this water so that I won't get thirsty and have to keep coming here to draw water."*

Jesus knows that the "Well" is a Symbol of endless, and unsatisfying desires, for the woman comes daily to the Well and yet gets thirsty again, but the water He will give will permanently quench her thirst because He is the Very Source of this Spring of endless, living Water.

St. Augustine says that human beings embark on a succession of desperate searches for earthly satisfaction / fulfillment / excessive pleasures: wealth and power, honor, false religions, philosophy, dissipation and distractions - futilities that only lead to obsession and addiction – the more you have, the less satisfied you are, and so you the more you seek. For Augustine, he was so weary of himself he could only cry out, *"you have made us for Yourself, O, Lord, and our heart is restless until it rests in You!"*

Jesus, knowing that this "Addictive Quality of Desire" is also what has defined the woman's relationships with men, tells her, "Go, call your husband and come back." "I have no husband," she replied.

Jesus said to her, "You are right when you say you have no husband. The fact is, you have had five husbands, and the man you now have is not your husband. What you have just said is quite true."

"Sir," the woman said, "I can see that you are a prophet. Our ancestors worshiped on this mountain, but you Jews claim that the place where we must worship is in Jerusalem."

"Woman," Jesus replied, "believe me, a time is coming when you will worship the Father neither on this mountain nor in Jerusalem…a time... has now come when the true worshipers will worship the Father in the Spirit and in truth...God is spirit, and his worshipers must worship in the Spirit and in truth."

The woman said, "I know that Messiah" (called Christ) "is coming. When he comes, he will explain everything to us."

Then Jesus declared, "I, the one speaking to you—**I am he**." I am the Messiah! **I Am**!

This is the blunt, commanding Voice of One who knows that Love carries responsibilities, and obligations. To whom much is given, much is expected. Having been made a Carrier of Living Water, the Samaritan woman is sent out on a Mission. As soon as she realizes who Jesus is and what he says He is – Messiah - the woman immediately puts down the water jar and goes into town to proclaim the message of the Living Water of everlasting Life to her people, *telling them:*

"Come, see a man who told me everything I ever did. Could this be the Messiah?"

They came out of the town and made their way toward him.

That Jar is the symbol of concupiscent, endless and

unsatisfying, worldly desires that is a futile effort and an attempt to assuage a hunger and a Thirst that is really Spiritual. Her Mission is now to evangelize others. She received a Gift of Spiritual healing, now, she must give back to others. This Law of the Gift: Love Begets Love, and Sacrifice. Now, the Woman of Samaria has become a Carrier of Living Water that heals, purifies and brings life to all; it is not stagnant water but Life-giving and flowing. **This Living Water is Love. And God is Love**, says St. John. Therefore, to be filled with Living Water is to be purified for Love, is to be filled with God, for God Is veritable Love.

Thus, the Woman of Samaria, by going out to proclaim the Good News (Gospel) of this Gift of flowing, Living Water of Love and Redemption to others, becomes the very first non-Jewish Apostle of Mission Evangelization.

The Fruits of her Evangelization are immediate

"Many of the Samaritans from that town believed in him because of the woman's testimony, 'He told me everything I ever did.'" So when the Samaritans came to him, they urged him to stay with them, and Jesus stayed two days. And because of his words, many more became believers.

They said to the woman, "We no longer believe just because of what you said; now we have heard for ourselves, and we know that this man really is the Savior of the world." (*John* 4: 4-42).

Bishop Robert Barron summarizes it thus:
"How wonderful that, having met the Source of Living

Water, she is able to set aside her addictions and to become, herself, a vehicle of healing for others. Pope St. John Paul II calls this, "The Law of the Gift." Bishop Barron reiterates, (very best definition of Evangelization that I've heard is this}:

'one starving person telling another starving person where to find bread [for]Demonstration of God's love should not be merely Abstract.'"

Thus, Love carries Responsibilities - Love is a concrete action of seeking the good of others. IT IS NOT MERELY A FEELING! Again, we see Trust in a pivotal role. The Woman of Samaria Trusted, and Obeyed, and thus became a Carrier of Living Water.

Equally, the stewards of the Wedding in Cana Trusted and acted on what Mary said to them: "Do Whatever He tells you to do." And Water was changed into the sweetest Wine.

Peter Trusted when our Lord, walking on waters, said to him: "Come!" Once he Trusted, he too walked on water, but when he stopped trusting, he started to sink. "Oh, ye of little Faith," the Lord reproached Peter.

At the Last Supper, when The Source of Living Water stooped to spray and wash the apostles' feet, Peter refused:

"No," said Peter, "you shall never wash my feet."

Jesus answered, "Unless I wash you, you have no part with me."

"Then, Lord," Simon Peter replied, "not just my feet, but my hands and my head as well!"

Trust is of such importance that The Lord himself on February 22, 1931 appeared to a young Polish nun named Sister Maria Faustyna Kowalska in a vision as Divine Mercy, with rays of mercy in the form of blood and water streaming forth from His Heart. He told her to paint an image of him and sign it, "Jesus, I Trust in You!" When the priest in Confession told her that Jesus meant that she should draw it in her own heart, Faustyna reported back to Jesus Who insisted, "I want you to paint it with paint. I am already painted in your heart." Jesus instructed that at the bottom of the Image be written, **"Jesus, I Trust in You!"** Faustyna did. To the Source of Living Water, "Trust" is cardinal.

Calling her the Secretary of His Mercy, He ordered her to also begin writing a Diary and to have instituted Mercy Sunday so others would come to know of his unfathomable Ocean of mercy. In a series of revelations that followed from 1931 through 1938, Jesus taught her about His unlimited ocean of mercy available to even the most hardened of sinners, saying "Let no soul fear to draw near to Me, even though its sins be as scarlet" (*Diary* 699) . . . . Whoever approaches the Fount of Life on this day will be granted complete forgiveness of sins and punishment" (*Diary* 300). Thus, still in pursuit of His created beings, through St. Faustyna, **Jesus offers to a World that is Thirsting for Peace the Instruments of Redemption: not just Water but His Blood, as well**.

Divine Mercy Sunday approved in the year 2,000 is strategically sandwiched between Crucifixion Friday and the Sunday after Easter Resurrection when practicing Catholics, if in a state of grace, must receive the Full splashing, cleansing and nourishment of Living Water.

When Jesus Died on the Cross, a soldier pierced his side and "Blood and Water" gushed out. God's mercy is an inexhaustible, bottomless Ocean of love and forgiveness, an Ocean of mercy not just flowing but gushing out, and so we say along with St. Faustyna,

"O Blood and Water which gush forth from the Heart of Jesus as a Fountain of mercy, I trust in You!"

* * * *

Mary of Nazareth: Model of Catholic Women

What are the attributes of Mary, our First Christian Woman? We find out through Self-examination.

We Catholic Christian Women should each ask ourselves – Are we Humble? If someone attacks us unjustly, spreads false stories against us, do we go fighting, ready to kill, or do we as Carriers of living Water who have received this Grace in the Blessed Eucharist, ponder about it as our Second Eve, Blessed Mary was wont to do? Do we pray about it, have patience and try and forgive? Forgiveness does not mean Reconciliation. although if Reconciliation poses great dangers to One, then, at least one should forgive with the Heart and pray for whoever.

Catholic Women, when we have the Living Water in us, should we quarrel? Are we patient with our husbands, guide them towards the Source of Living Water? Do we quarrel and fight with family members, with fellow market sellers, even with our priests?

Priests Dispenser of Grace/Living Water

Do we realize that a Priest is a Dispenser of Grace, and of Living Water?

David honored Saul and refused to have him killed, even when he had cornered him because the King has been anointed with the oil of the Lord. St. Francis of Assisi would stoop and kiss the hand of a sinful priest, made a pariah by other people, because the Priest's sinfulness and unworthiness as a man do not nullify his Spiritual Duty as the One to hand to us the Body and Blood of Jesus in the Holy Eucharist, as still the one to be the instrument of our receiving Living Water.

As Christian Women, should we look at our Catholic Women Organization offices as a mere money-making opportunity, or as a medium to honestly, humbly, trustingly serve the Lord just as Mary did?

When Mary of Galilee agreed to be Carrier of Living Word, what did she do? Straightaway, aware of the Law of the Gift, she went to visit her older cousin Elizabeth, to clean for her, and serve her so they can praise and adore the Lord their God Together. Elizabeth recognized the Source of Living Water resident in Mary because her own babe-in-the-womb, John, having been splashed and purified, leapt up for Joy in recognition and adoration of The Word, causing his mother Elizabeth to Hail Mary: "Blessed are you among Women, and Blessed is the fruit of your womb. How is it that the mother of my Lord has come to me!" And Mary agrees, recognizing God's singular honor to her:

"From now, all generations shall call me 'Blessed!" (*The Magnificat*) Ah yes, Today and Always, Catholic Women Carriers of the Living Water do call and shall always call Mary "Blessed." Like Mary, do we try to live the Eight (8) Beatitudes? (*Matthew* 5: 1-12).

Like Mary, do we visit those in difficult circumstances, those who are sick and old? Those who are in prison, and comfort those in sorrow?

Do we, as Pope Francis I insists, go out to the Field Hospitals of the Wounded to minister to them?

In the home and in our communities, do we Catholic Women as Carriers of Living Water live out the Marian Model of Christian Motherhood as Mary of Galilee did?

Do we truly love our husbands as Mary loved Joseph, and strive to be faithful to our marriage vows; do we guide our husbands right, encouraging them to live a proper, Christian Values-oriented lives?

Do we train our children - daughters and sons - to have proper Christly and Family values just like Mary trained Jesus to be - honest, hardworking, generous, and to have love for God and their neighbors?

Do we spend quality leisurely time with our children, to make them Trust us enough to come to us when they are in trouble? Do we try to find out who their friends, and associates are? Do we ask questions when they bring unwarranted and expensive things which we know did not come from us, the parents? Do we lovingly reprimand / discipline them, if, and when we have to, so they can learn their lessons at home rather than in prison, or in Juvenile Correction centers?

Do we Catholic Women, Carriers of Living Water, pray as a Family with our husband and children? Do we Teach them the Catholic Catechism, Catholic Doctrines and the Sacraments?

Do we prepare our children to be God-fearing and compassionate future social, economic and political leaders of our Society?

Do we, Catholic Women live out the Model of Christian Womanbeing as Mary of Galilee did: Self-disciplined, Self-respecting? Catholic Women Carriers of Living Water, are we pure at heart, chaste in our bodies - the temple of God - so we can worship God in the Spirit and in Truth just as the Source of Living Water told the Woman of Samaria, and she at once laid down her pot of fleshly concupiscence, and went on her evangelizing ministry?

Do we, as Catholic Women, Carriers of Living Water, try to maintain silence interiorly sometimes; and if we are confronted with challenges we do not understand, imitate our model Mary, Jesus' Mother and ponder these in our hearts, or do we talk endlessly, spreading gossip, and slandering fellow women, and sowing discord in our communities?

Would Mary have done some of the things we do everyday? We Must daily ask ourselves these hard questions, examine our conscience for spiritual Discernment, and behave as proper Carriers of *Living Water which comes from "I Am Who Am" – Jesus, in the co-equal, co-eternal Trinitarian bond with the Father, and the Spirit!*

* * * *

Catholic Women as Carriers of Living Water

What to do? Where to Start? How?

Jesus memorialized His Being as the Sacrificial Lamb of God at the Last Supper when He offered up His body for the sake of Love: "Then he took a cup, and giving thanks, He gave it to them, saying, *"Drink from it, all of you. This is my blood of the covenant which is poured out for many for the forgiveness of sins"* (*Matthew* 26: 27-29) - Our Sins! On the Cross, the very Source of Living Water cried out, *"I Thirst!."*

He was and is Always thirsting for our Love. So, at Mass, we receive, in form of bread and wine, in Eucharistic Form – the real Body and Blood of the Lord Jesus. He, the Source of Living Water is offering to us His real Body and Blood. So, we Catholics, all Christians, especially Catholic Women who daily receive the Body and Blood, purified, nourished and made Holy, we as Carriers of Living Water hear the priest say to us: *"Ite Missa est* = Mass is ended – so, carry this Divine Life of graces to others in our Communities.

Missio is nominative for S*ending out*

First used by Jesuit missionaries who would send their members overseas to teach, establish schools and hospitals. Also, humanitarian workers are habitually sent out on a mission – *missio*. The Resurrected Lord Jesus before Ascension tells His Disciples, "Go Forth, I am sending you out to preach to all nations...." - Meaning that both Jesus and the priest are not telling Catholic Women to carry the Living Water, gifted to them by its Source, and hide its fruits just as the Servant with the one talent did who buried it and got cursed out by his Master.

Talent in Hebraic tradition is not really money, but a Shining, heavy weighty object that is precious, meant for Sacrifice – for Giving out. It symbolizes Living Grace meant not to be hoarded but to be passed on, to be Gifted to others, too. Both Christ and the priest are saying, "I am sending you abroad in your communities on a Mission to now Carry this Living Water springing from the Source of Love and Eternal Life and go splash abroad its Graces so it can Purify, Energize, Revitalize, and Shine on others, too.

As Catholic Women, Carriers of Living Water, may we end our conversation with the prayer of Blessed Cardinal John Henry Newman, which was adopted and popularized by St. Mother Teresa of Calcutta:

"Dear Jesus, help me to spread Your fragrance everywhere I go.
Flood my soul with Your spirit and life.
Penetrate and possess my whole being so utterly,
That my life may only be a radiance of Yours.

Shine through me and be so in me
That every soul I come in contact with
May feel Your presence in my soul.
Let them look up and see no longer me, but only Jesus!
Stay with me and then I shall begin to shine as You shine,
So to shine as to be a light to others;
The light, O Jesus will be all from You; none of it will be mine;
It will be you, shining on others through me.
Let me thus praise You the way You love best,
By shining on those around me.
Let me preach You without preaching, not by words but by my example,
By the catching force of the sympathetic influence of what I do,
The evident fullness of the love my heart bears to You...."
Amen.

(Bl. John Henry Newman 1801-1890)

So, beloved Catholic Women Carriers of Living Water, we are on a **"Shining forth Mission of Service"** to bring our Gift of Living Water to a World that is Thirsty for Peace. We are on a Mission for as Bl. John Henry Newman again reminds us:

"God has created me to do Him some definite service. He has committed some work to me which He has not committed to another. I have my mission. I may never know it in this life, but I shall be told it in the next. I am a link in a chain, a bond of connection between persons....
He has not created me for naught. I shall do good; I shall do His work.

I shall be an angel of peace, a preacher of truth in my own place, while not intending it if I do but keep His commandments. Therefore, I will Trust Him, whatever I am: I can never be thrown away: If I am in sickness, my sickness may serve Him; in perplexity, my perplexity may serve Him. If I am in sorrow, my sorrow may serve Him. He does nothing in vain. He knows what He is about. He may take away my friends. He may throw me among strangers. He may make me feel desolate, make my spirits sink, hide my future from me. Still, He knows what He is about."

Thus, with God, it is all about Trust to be a true Carrier of Living Water to our World that Thirsts for Peace.

Notes:

Missio: Pope Francis, St. Ignatius of Loyola, St. Francis Xavier, etc. are all Jesuits of the Society of Jesus.

Dr. Rose Ure Mezu was born in Nigeria and studied in Port-Harcourt, (Nigeria), Abidjan, (Côte d'Ivoire), Buffalo (New York) and Paris (France) where she graduated with a Diplôme d'Etudes from the Sorbonne. She obtained a Ph.D. in Comparative Literature in 1993, specializing in Francophone and Anglo-phone Feminist Literature. She had been a Commissioner of Social Welfare in Imo State, Nigeria, and Professor of English, Women Studies and Comparative Literature at Morgan State University, Baltimore, Maryland, USA. She is also the founder and Co-ordinator of WADS: Black Creativity & the State of the Race, which organizes international and interdisciplinary conferences on Africa and the Diaspora. A widely published scholar, her books include *Women in Chains: Abandonment in Love Relationships in the Fiction of Selected West African Writers* (1994), *Songs of the Hearth* (1993), *Homage to my People* (2004), *A History of Africana Women's Literature* (2004), and with Dr S. Okechukwu Mezu, *Black Nationalists: Reconsidering Du Bois, Garvey, Booker T. & Nkrumah* (1999); *John Paul II and Africa* (2005); *Africa and the Diaspora: The Black Scholar and Society* (1999); *Religion and Society* (1999); *Writers of African Descent Speak: Black Creativity and the State of the Race – Leadership, Culture, and Racism* (1998); *Chinua Achebe: The Man and His Works*(2005).

Black Academy Press, Inc.
4015 Old Court Road
Baltimore, Maryland 21208
http://blackacademypress.com/

Printed in the United States of America

www.ingramcontent.com/pod-product-compliance
Lightning Source LLC
LaVergne TN
LVHW010022070426
835508LV00001B/9